DATE DUE

Essential Lives

MARGARET MEAD

Essential Lives

MARGARET MEAD

CULTURAL ANTHROPOLOGIST

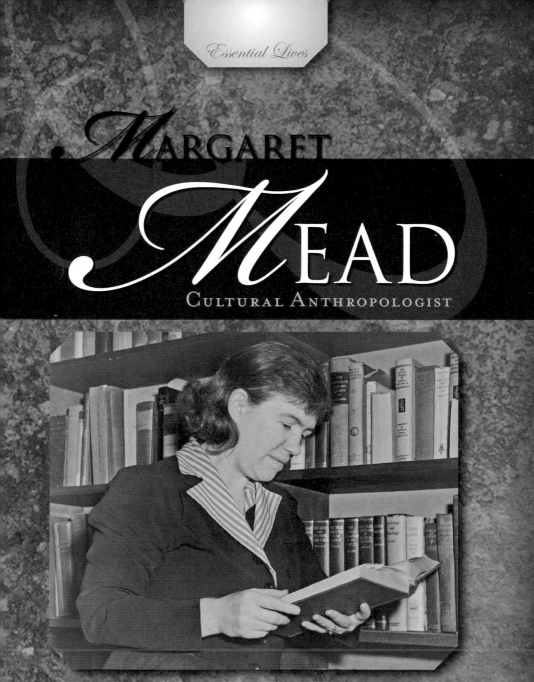

by Ruth Strother

Content Consultant:
Maija Sedzielarz, Coordinator, School Visit Programs,
Science Museum of Minnesota

ABDO
Publishing Company

CREDITS

Published by ABDO Publishing Company, 8000 West 78th Street, Edina, Minnesota 55439. Copyright © 2009 by Abdo Consulting Group, Inc. International copyrights reserved in all countries. No part of this book may be reproduced in any form without written permission from the publisher. The Essential Library™ is a trademark and logo of ABDO Publishing Company.

Printed in the United States.

Editor: Jill Sherman
Copy Editor: Paula Lewis
Interior Design and Production: Emily Love
Cover Design: Emily Love

Library of Congress Cataloging-in-Publication Data
Strother, Ruth.
  Margaret Mead : cultural anthropologist / by Ruth Strother.
      p. cm. — (Essential lives)
  Includes bibliographical references and index.
  ISBN 978-1-60453-525-9
  1. Mead, Margaret, 1901-1978. 2. Anthropologists—United States—Biography. 3. Women anthropologists—United States—Biography. 4. Ethnology—Melanesia. 5. Melanesia—Social life and customs. I. Title.

  GN21.M36S87 2009
  306.092—dc22
  [B]

                        2008033498

TABLE OF CONTENTS

Margaret Mead, 1940

FIRSTS

In 1925, the first television was introduced to the world, a woman was elected governor for the first time, and Margaret Mead took her first step onto the soil of Pago Pago, the capital of American Samoa. The cultural observations that Mead made and recorded helped her become one of the most famous anthropologists in the United States. Her work brought the field of anthropology into the minds of ordinary Americans, who realized that they could see pieces of themselves in other very different societies.

STARTING OUT

Margaret Mead took an interest in studying anthropology as an undergraduate student at Barnard College at Columbia University. She thought that anthropology would help her understand the confusing world in which she lived. America was moving away from the rigid Victorian era of the late nineteenth century into a new, less restrictive way of life. The Roaring Twenties, the Jazz Age, and the Age of Wonderful Nonsense all refer to the 1920s. Life in the United States was changing quickly—goods were being mass-produced, women were voting for the first time, and a new form of transportation, the

Anthropology

Anthropology is the study of customs, values, language, and beliefs shared by people living together in a community. Although anthropology had already been around for approximately 100 years, it was still a relatively new field of study in the 1920s.

As stated in Jane Howard's *Margaret Mead: A Life*, "Anthropology . . . could free a civilization from its own prejudices and encourage it to 'apply standards in measuring our achievements that have a greater absolute truth than those derived from a study of our civilization alone.'"[1]

automobile, was gaining in popularity. And yet, there was a dark side to these times. Strict laws known as Prohibition banned the sale and consumption of alcohol and tempted many people to break the law. These laws also encouraged gangsters such as Al Capone to illegally sell and distribute liquor.

Columbia University was a good place to study anthropology in the 1920s. The school was home to famed anthropologist Franz Boas. Mead attended Boas's lectures and found them to be inspirational. Before long, her interest in anthropology turned into fascination. Mead decided to study anthropology for a doctorate degree (PhD).

As a PhD student, Mead worked closely with Boas. In order to write her dissertation, she had to conduct field research. Mead wanted to travel to Polynesia and study remote people and cultures that had never been exposed to Western culture. However, Boas thought she should stay in the United States. Boas was concerned about Mead being isolated on a remote Polynesian island. Mead had never traveled out of the country before. On this trip,

"I have spent most of my life studying the lives of other peoples, faraway peoples, so that Americans might better understand themselves."[2]

—*Margaret Mead*

Franz Boas

she would be traveling alone to a place where she did not speak the language.

Determined to conduct her fieldwork in Polynesia, Mead reached a compromise with Boas. She proposed to complete her research in American Samoa, a group of Polynesian islands in the South

Pacific. Samoa was a regular stop for boats bringing supplies to American military personnel stationed there. This meant Mead would not be completely isolated, which met with Boas's approval. Many of the interior villages remained mostly untouched by outside influences, so Mead was satisfied as well.

Mead also agreed to study Boas's topic of choice: the adolescent girl. Boas believed that behavior is shaped by society and culture and not just by biology, which was the more popular belief among anthropologists at that time. He was especially interested in how the rules of society affected adolescent girls. Do they rebel, as they do in the United States, or do they meekly accept the restrictions? Mead agreed to the study of adolescent girls as a starting point. She broadened her study to include how culture was passed down to children and how cultural expectations differed between males and females.

"Of So Great Glee"

Margaret Mead wrote poetry throughout her life. When she knew she would be conducting her research in Samoa, she was absolutely gleeful and wrote a poem titled "Of So Great Glee." The final stanza reads, "And when at last she tore a star / Out of the studded sky, / God only smiled at one whose glee / Could fling a rope so high."[3]

At that time, anthropologists had made few studies on the topic of women and children, and fieldwork was still in its infancy. Mead had to determine how to conduct her research. Boas suspected that Mead's work would make an impact on ethnology—the study, systematic recording, and scientific description of the customs of human culture.

Pago Pago

At the end of August 1925, Mead docked on Pago Pago on the island of Tutuila. Mead was utterly alone.

"Papa Franz"

Known as the father of American anthropology, Franz Boas was born in Minden, Germany, on July 8, 1858. His most famous anthropological mission was in 1886 to study the Kwakiutl Indians of the Canadian Pacific Coast.

Boas was Columbia University's first anthropology professor. Students were drawn to him and the field of anthropology. He was a mentor to many who became well-known experts in anthropology, including Margaret Mead. A father figure, he was called "Papa Franz" by some of his students. Boas imparted knowledge and some direction to his students, but he did not prepare them for fieldwork.

Shortly before Mead was to set off for Samoa, Papa Franz gave her some fatherly advice in a letter dated July 14, 1925:

My dear Margaret,

I suppose the time is drawing near when you want to leave. Let me impress upon you once more first of all that you should not forget your health. I am sure you will be careful in the tropics and try to adjust yourself to conditions and not work when it is too hot and moist in the daytime. If you find that you cannot stand the climate do not be ashamed to come back. There are plenty of other places where you could solve the same problem on which you propose to work.[4]

Samoa is in relative isolation in the Pacific Ocean.

She did not know where she would conduct her
fieldwork, but she had a letter of introduction from
the surgeon general of the navy. As a result, a young
English-speaking Samoan nurse was assigned the task
of teaching Mead the native language.

After weeks of waiting, Mead received a check as
part of the funding for her research. She was finally
able to pay her hotel bill and set off for the village
of Vaitogi. There, Mead stayed at a chief's house for
ten days and became friends with his daughter. Mead
learned much about Samoan etiquette in order to

experience the culture as closely as possible. She also participated in many of the rituals and customs. To Mead, participation was just as important as observation for her research.

THE FIELDWORK BEGINS

Mead decided on her ultimate destination: the Manua Islands, specifically the island of Tau. Remote and nearly untouched by the outside world, Tau seemed a good choice for Mead's fieldwork. And to lessen Boas's concerns, she was near a medical post in Tau that was occupied by a navy man and his family. Mead set up her "home" on the porch of the clinic.

These living arrangements suited Mead. Although she felt she should be living in a Samoan household, she did not care for the idea of sitting on a dirt floor in a house without exterior walls. In a

Four Fields of Anthropology

Franz Boas helped establish the four fields of anthropology: linguistics, archeology, physical anthropology, and cultural anthropology. Linguistics is the study of language and how it is used to pass the culture from one generation to the next. Archeology uses human remains and artifacts to learn about long-ago human cultures. Physical anthropology takes a biological approach by focusing on adaptations and evolution of humans. Cultural anthropology focuses on the customs of social groups, their laws, structures, technology, and art.

letter dated December 11, 1925, about a month after she had arrived in Tau, Mead wrote:

> *There is the most peculiar sensation one gets here from even a few hours in a native house, a different taste in the mouth, a sense of heavy, almost sticky heat, a feeling as if one's skin were going to fly off in thin gossamer layers and a curious buzzing inside one's head, mostly from the strain of listening. I don't know exactly what is responsible for it, possibly the food and sitting cross-legged and the flies.*[5]

Mead spent approximately nine months studying adolescent girls in Samoa. She used her background in psychology to conduct psychological tests as well as anthropological observations. Her studies showed that, unlike Western cultures, adolescence was not a stressful time for Samoan girls. Mead concluded that culture, not biology, determined behavior. Mead's findings supported Boas's theory.

The Popularization of Anthropology

After nine months of study in Samoa, Mead returned to the United States. There, she accepted the job of assistant curator at the American Museum of Natural History. She gave lectures, worked on her PhD dissertation, titled *An Inquiry into the Question of*

Cultural Stability in Polynesia, and started writing her first book, *Coming of Age in Samoa*.

This marked the first time an anthropologist had written a book about her field research for a general, nonacademic audience. The first publisher she sent her book to rejected it, but it was later accepted by William Morrow. Based on his suggestions, Mead added chapters that focused on how her findings could be applied to raising and educating children in the United States. This personal application to U.S. readers along with Mead's nonacademic, vivid, almost poetic account of Samoan life made *Coming of Age in Samoa* a success.

No one could have predicted the impact this book would have, or what this book would do for anthropology and for Margaret Mead. As more people became

Nature versus Nurture

During the mid-1920s, the relative importance of "nature versus nurture" was debated. The question centered on how much personality and behavior were guided by biology, or a person's inborn tendencies (nature), and how much was guided by culture, or the society in which a person lives (nurture). A definitive answer has yet to be made; the nature versus nurture debate continues.

familiar with Mead's work, they began to wonder how much of a person's identity is due to the culture and society in which they live. As people were beginning to consider the questions raised by Mead's book, it was not long before *Margaret Mead* and *anthropology* became household words. ⌣

A Samoan house

Emily Mead with daughter Margaret

ANCESTORS OF AN
ANTHROPOLOGIST

The Mead family had a long history of strong, smart women even before Margaret Mead entered the family. The presence of strong, independent women set a precedent for future generations. The Meads tried hard to provide their children with the skills, knowledge, and life experiences that would prepare them for success.

THE FOGGS

James Leland Fogg was a successful merchant living in the Midwest. He married Elizabeth Bogart. Together they had five children. James died in 1903 when his grandchildren were still young. In his absence, his daughter Emily tried to live by her father's motto, "Do good because it is right to do good." Emily took his motto so seriously that she would live by it her entire life and teach her children to live by it as well.

Though Elizabeth Bogart Fogg remarried after her husband's death, she continued to visit her adult children. However, she did not have a very close relationship with her grandchildren.

Woodrow Wilson

When she was very young, Mead's family lived in a cottage next door to Woodrow Wilson, before he became president of the United States. After Wilson became president, Mead remarked, "I liked to remember that he, too, had seen me as a baby. Somehow I got the feeling that my sense of having been seen by important persons lay back of my ease in public appearances and my enjoyment in being recognized as myself."[1]

The Meads

Martha Adaline Ramsay grew up in Winchester, Ohio, which had been founded by her grandfathers. Martha's father was a jack-of-all-trades and worked as a farmer, a justice of the peace, and a Methodist preacher, among other occupations.

In the late 1800s, most women did not work outside the home, but Martha Ramsay taught school. She taught students in all grades but especially liked teaching the younger students.

Letter to Grandmother from Samoa

Sweet little Grandma,

I've just been reading one of your Atlantic Monthly*'s with a big penciled cross on the table of contents. . . . The pencil mark was against Kuble's article on "Participating in the Grand Adventure." And I thought how really wonderful it is to have a grand-mother of over 80 who would mark an article like that. Probably that is one of the reasons that my life has been such a se-rene untroubled development. I not only had no quarrel with the essential thought of my parents, but I also had none with that of my grandmother—a very rare privi-lege in as changing an age as ours. All the energy which most of my contemporaries had to put into reconciling affection for their elders with honest revolt against their teachings, I could conserve to use for my own development. It's very much owing to you that I've wasted so little time in life, made so few false moves, chased so few chimeras, extraneous to my personality.*

The Samoans always thought that the most remarkable thing about me was that my father's mother, over 80, was still living. And, put into less material terms, I think they were very right.

Lovingly, Margaret [2]

She married another teacher, Giles Mead, and the two headed off to college together. Giles became an innovative and well-regarded school superintendent. They had one child together, Edward. Giles died in 1880 while still a young man. Edward was just six years old at the time of his father's death.

Martha Mead, now a widow with a young boy to raise, continued to teach. Martha taught until Edward married Emily Fogg in 1900, and then she moved into their house. Martha lived with her son's family for the rest of her life. She never remarried.

Martha took a central position in the household. Her room was the gathering place for family and friends. She was strong and self-assured, and she demanded respect. When she wanted something done, she never pleaded with her grandchildren, she never

The Setup

Mead felt she grew up ahead of her time. She said this was partly because "during my whole childhood I shared my grandmother's lively relationship to the past and the present. But it was also because I was the child of social scientists who were deeply—and differently—concerned with the state of the world. For me, being brought up to become a woman who could live responsibly in the contemporary world and learning to become an anthropologist, conscious of the culture in which I lived, were almost the same thing."[3]

threatened them, and she never screamed at them. She expected them to obey, and they did.

Parents

Edward Mead and Emily Fogg were academics. They met at the University of Chicago in 1896, while Emily was working toward her undergraduate degree. Edward was working on his PhD in political economics. Shortly after their first meeting, Edward knew that Emily was the woman he should marry.

Edward Mead became a teacher at the Wharton School of Finance and Commerce at the University of Pennsylvania. He worked his way up to a full professor and the chairman of Wharton's evening extension school. A hardworking man, he believed in trust and loyalty and the importance of contributing new information to one's chosen field of study. At the time, the U.S. monetary system was based on the value of gold. As an economist, he became interested in gold and gold mining and wrote *The Story of Gold*.

Edward Mead was often aloof and kept his feelings to himself. One of his favorite leisure pastimes was to read mystery novels. Although his specialty was finance and the economy, he did not earn much money. While Edward did not interact often with his children, he was sometimes overprotective and feared for their safety. He tried to limit their physical activity as much as possible.

At six feet (1.8 m), Edward was one foot (0.3 m) taller than his wife. His nickname for her was Tiny Wife. But other than her stature, there was not much else "tiny" about Emily Mead. Emily was a practical, intellectual, and ambitious person. She was not much interested in the little pleasures in life. For Emily,

> *Life was real, life was earnest—it was too serious for trivial things. She had babies to care for and a house to manage. She also felt it was important to continue her own intellectual life and to be a responsible citizen in a world in which there were many wrongs—wrongs to the poor and the downtrodden, to foreigners, to Negroes, to women—that had to be set right.* [4]

Emily Mead was among those who believed that the social sciences

The Gold Standard

Initially used from 1879 to 1914 by many countries, the gold standard was a monetary system. Gold is too heavy to carry around everywhere, so it was decided that paper bills could be used as currency. Paper, however, has little value. To make paper bills worth something, they needed to be tied to a worthy resource—such as gold. The bills would represent an agreed-upon amount of gold.

Female Solidarity

Margaret Mead once said that "the strongest feeling in their household . . . was a rule of absolute solidarity among women. The pattern in the families [my mother and grandmothers] came from, as in many others in America, was for charming, potentially caddish men, men who needed indulgence and forgiveness, to mate with stern, impressive women who took charge and took care."[5]

could solve the problems of society. She was granted a fellowship from Bryn Mawr College, which allowed her to continue her sociological research on families of Italian immigrants. The Meads moved often to accommodate Emily's research and her various academic pursuits.

Margaret Mead's upbringing prepared her for
her future as an anthropologist.

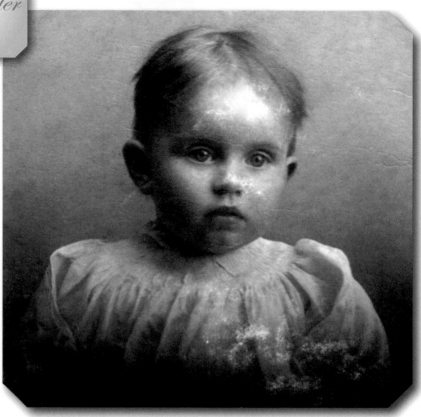

Margaret Mead, 1902

THE EARLY YEARS

One year after their marriage, Emily Mead gave birth to a daughter. Margaret Mead was born on December 16, 1901, in Philadelphia, Pennsylvania. In the early twentieth century, most children were born at home, but Margaret was born at the West Park Hospital. She also had the distinction of being the very first child born at that hospital.

When Emily discovered that she was pregnant, she began to keep a daily journal. She believed that her experiences and moods during pregnancy would have an effect on her baby. As a sociologist, Emily Mead was trained to observe people. She continued keeping her journal well after Margaret was born. Although it was common for a mother to keep track of her child's development and milestones, Emily Mead took it a bit further. She filled 13 notebooks chronicling Margaret's early years.

Margaret not only had a unique start to her life, but her home life was much different from that of the average child. For instance, instead of sleeping in a crib, she slept in a Morris chair, a large easy chair with arms and an adjustable back. She had strong women role models and a grandparent who lived with the family. She was homeschooled and exposed to academics and social issues. Looking back on her childhood, Margaret wrote,

> *I took pride in being unlike other children and in living in a household that was itself unique. But at the same time I longed to share in every culturally normal experience.*[1]

A Brother

Margaret's father nicknamed her Punk. He called her Punk until she was two years old, when in 1904 her little brother, Richard, was born. Richard then inherited the nickname Punk, and Margaret became the Original Punk. Margaret's father had little involvement in raising his children, but he showed them affection and tried to be a strong male role model.

Richard was often ill and not as robust as Margaret,

From Emily Mead's Notebooks

Transcription of "Characteristics at 6 Years":

1.) affectionate

2.) wishes to be helpful

3.) Fond of Richard but selfish to him (when he went up for operation and did not come back, wept and was inconsolable)

4.) continually asking questions. What is that? What does that word mean?

5.) always busy at something

6.) very bright + original

7.) curious

8.) expresses herself very well

9.) tantrums consist of much impertinent talking or (when Mother waving hands) stamping feet, etc.

10.) great determination + perseverance when wants anything

11.) not orderly but willing to pick up

12.) Fond of outdoor life

13.) Social - anxious for companionship, but plays well alone.

14.) Some sense of humor Likes jokes

15.) Soon repentant

16.) Likes to get best of people.[2]

---

which sometimes made their father overprotective. At times, Margaret was allowed to participate in rough-and-tumble activities from which Richard was banned. But Margaret's memories of her early childhood consistently included her brother. She remembered doing everything with him—except singing. Richard had a beautiful singing voice, and Margaret did not.

Margaret had one complaint about Richard: He always told the truth. If he tried to lie, his face would turn bright red with the falseness of his words. Margaret was mischievous and wished for an older brother who would "be a ringleader in positive wickedness."[3]

SISTERS

Though still a child, Margaret was often treated like an adult by the adults in her household. Margaret felt that her thoughts and opinions were weighed as heavily as any adult's in the household.

When Margaret was four years old she was given the privilege of naming her baby sister. Margaret chose the name Katherine. Margaret found everything her baby sister did to be delightful, even the way she pulled off her socks. The family was distraught when nine-month-old Katherine suddenly died in 1907.

In 1909, Emily Mead gave birth to another child, Elizabeth. Emily Mead had been sick during this pregnancy, and Elizabeth was a frail infant. Margaret said she did not

> *know whether it was our doubt that she would stay with us or whether it was her vividness and charm that so captivated me, but I felt that she had been sent to take the place of the baby who had died.*[4]

Favorites

Margaret's sister Priscilla wrote, "Dick was Dadda's favorite, Elizabeth was Grandma's favorite, Margaret was everybody's favorite. I was Mother's favorite, but Mother didn't count for much in our house."[5]

A short 18 months after Elizabeth's birth, Priscilla was born. Just as Margaret and Richard were paired during their childhood, so were Elizabeth and Priscilla.

Emily Mead had kept a journal when Richard was born, as she had with Margaret, but had filled only four notebooks with her observations. Now, there were two younger girls in the family. Grandma Mead made it eight-year-old Margaret's responsibility to observe her baby sisters' behavior

and development by keeping a
journal. It was not long before
Margaret began to think of her little
sisters as her children.

Moving Around

The Meads moved often—
about twice a year. The first city
Margaret remembers calling home
was Hammonton, New Jersey,
where her mother studied Italian
immigrants. The Meads generally
spent the spring and fall in
Hammonton. In the winter, they
lived in or around Philadelphia to accommodate
Edward's teaching schedule.

As they constantly moved, someone in the Mead
household had to keep track of important family
information, such as medical histories and names
and addresses of friends and neighbors from the
various places they lived. That person was Margaret.
Her childhood taught her to be an observer and
chronicler of life.

At every new house they moved into, Margaret
claimed the room farthest away from the others as

> "Margaret . . . grew up with two strong convictions: that being observed was wonderful, and that observing others, far from being anything to feel guilty about, was more wonderful still."[6]
>
> —*Jane Howard,*
> *Margaret Mead: A Life*

Priscila wants some food.

I thought mother up third floor.

Get out of my way.

No no rock me, I rock dolly, dolly comes first.

I feed my dolly, my dolly hungry.

I had button hook yesterday.

I wipe my nose, my nose running.

Margaret Mead's record of her sister Elizabeth's language development her own; if it was on the top floor, it was even better. She wanted plenty of warning in the form of footsteps when someone was approaching. The next order of business was to explore the new house to discover all its nooks and crannies so she would be ready for the next game of hide-and-seek.

When Margaret was ten years old in 1911, the Meads moved to an old 18-room farmhouse on 107 acres (43.3 ha) in Holicong, Pennsylvania. There were fields of grain and corn. The various animals included a bull and six horses. In the triple-story barn, Margaret produced plays. The farm offered great fun and adventure for Margaret. And yet, she was quite restless during this time. Country life was predictable and she wanted more challenges and more excitement. She began to investigate religious beliefs and practices.

Hiding Away

The tradition of finding a room far from others to hide away in followed Margaret into her adult years. After her research in Samoa, Mead took a job at the American Museum of Natural History in New York City. There, she was given an attic office. "It was just like the room I had at the farm and the kind of room I had always chosen in each rented house we lived in. Among other advantages, there were two stairways leading up to the tower, just as there had been in all the better houses we had rented; this meant that one could creep down one stairway while someone whom one did not want to meet—in my childhood, my mother or the person who was It in a game, or later, a too solicitous elderly curator—was coming up the other."[7]

Harvesting Wheat

The farm that the Meads moved into was a working farm. Margaret's father showed her how he had learned to top off bundles of wheat during his childhood in Ohio. He then gave her the task of instructing the threshers, men who had come to work on the farm, without angering them.

Religion was not a part of the Mead household, but Margaret's parents had allowed her to go with neighbors to their churches and Sunday schools. Margaret already had established her religious beliefs and faith; she was looking for a way to practice her faith and for rituals to ground her in her faith. Eventually, Margaret found an Episcopal church in Buckingham, Pennsylvania, that suited her. A few days before her eleventh birthday, Margaret was baptized. ⁓

Margaret and Richard Mead, 1911

Margaret Mead, self-portrait, age 13

THE SCHOOL YEARS

Most children would find the kind of schooling Margaret Mead received from her grandma and mother too good to be true. Margaret spent just one hour a day learning indoors. Then, she played outside and explored nature for the rest of the day. It was a school regime that suited Margaret but had some drawbacks as well.

LEARNING AT HOME

Margaret was homeschooled for much of her education. The Meads thought elementary school was a waste of time. Grandma Mead had taught in schools for most of her life and had especially strong opinions about education. She believed that children should not have to sit still for more than an hour; memorizing and drilling facts was a worthless use of time. Instead, Grandma Mead favored active and informative learning. For example, she would send Margaret outside to analyze and classify plants. Grandma Mead taught Margaret how to observe nature and note her observations. However, there were drawbacks to Grandma Mead's way of teaching, too—Margaret never learned to spell well.

While Grandma Mead taught the more academic subjects, Emily

Notes on Margaret's School Day

Grandma Mead kept notes on her grandchildren's progress. These are some notes she took during Margaret Mead's school days:

"Sept. 29. 'Margaret made figures with corn and then drew them on paper.'

Oct. 23. 'We found a robin's nest in the grape arbor. There were pieces of the frail shells showing the "Robin's egg blue". I asked M. the color. She said 'green', which is almost correct.'

Oct. 23. 'She is continually drawing from her store of Literature, and adapting it.'"[1]

Mead took charge of giving Margaret experience in
the arts. In the various neighborhoods they lived
in, Emily Mead found skilled craftspeople to teach
an aspect of art to her children. Margaret learned
painting, music, woodcarving, basketry, and even
how to build a loom.

Looking back on her education, Margaret Mead
wrote,

> [I]t seems to me that this way of organizing teaching and
> learning around special skills provided me with a model
> for the way I have always organized work, whether it has
> involved organizing a research team, a staff of assistants, or
> the available informants in a native village. In every case I try
> to find out what each person is good at doing and then I fit
> them together in a group that forms some kind of whole.[2]

Formal School

When Margaret was nine years old, the Meads
were living in Swarthmore, Pennsylvania, and
Margaret was sent to the local public school for
fourth grade. However, the class was not held in
a typical classroom. As a result of an unexpected
increase in enrollment, the school district rented
a room in the town hall for the fourth-grade class.

The hall was rented only for half-days, so the fourth-grade day was shortened accordingly.

Many aspects of school were easy for Margaret, but some were more difficult. She nearly failed fourth-grade arithmetic. But three months later, she was excelling. She started writing poetry, a pastime she would continue well into her adult years. She also wrote some short plays and began keeping a diary. After just one year of formal schooling, Margaret decided to go back to her grandmother's lessons at home.

Margaret again attended school for eighth grade. This time, Margaret attended a private school, the Buckingham Friends School, run by Quakers. The teachers did not quite know what to do with her. When they called on her to answer a question, she monopolized the class until the end of the period. School did not work out well for Margaret

"In all the schools I had attended so far I felt as if I were in some way taking part in a theatrical performance in which I had a role to play and had to find actors to take the other parts."[3]

—*Margaret Mead*

An entry from Mead's childhood diary

that year and she was homeschooled again during her
freshman year in high school.

In 1916, when Margaret was 15 years old, the
Meads moved to Doylestown, Pennsylvania. Margaret
entered the public high school as a sophomore.
She did not quite fit in with the other students,
but she did try to become involved with high school
life. Writing was an important part of Margaret's

life, so she helped start the school magazine. Margaret's social life received a big boost when the Meads opened their house to the community and hosted a dance the first Saturday of every month.

"Writing was what my parents did, and writing was as much a part of my life as gardening and canning were in the life of a farmer's daughter of that day."[4]

—*Margaret Mead*

Another high school project that occupied Margaret was a five-poster exhibit she created. Each poster represented a theme: womanhood, childhood, visions, religion, and internationalism. Each of these themes would become an important focus in her future work as an anthropologist.

LUTHER CRESSMAN

Emily Mead invited one of Margaret's teachers, George Cressman, for dinner during the weekend he was to give the high school commencement speech. His 20-year-old brother Luther was visiting for the weekend and was invited as well. That same evening, 16-year-old Margaret and the dashing, redheaded Luther danced through the night at a high school dance. After the festivities, Margaret had an appendicitis attack. She was unable to see Luther again until the following fall. By Christmas 1917,

Luther had asked Margaret to marry him. However, the couple kept their engagement a secret from their families.

Margaret was not able to attend Luther's college graduation because she had the measles. She did not know when she would be able to see him again. The United States was in the midst of World War I. Luther was in the Reserve Officer's Training Corps (ROTC) and attended training camp in 1917, while Margaret stayed home and rolled bandages for the Red Cross. When the war ended in 1918, Luther came home and the couple announced their engagement.

Luther wanted to be a minister. This choice pleased Margaret. She thought a minister's wife would be a good life for her. She did suggest that he change his religion from Lutheran to Episcopalian, though. In 1919, Luther took Margaret's suggestion, changed his religion, and started school at the General Theological Seminary in New York City.

Although she did not get to see Luther as often as she might have liked during their engagement, Margaret was happy with their relationship. She did not have to worry about dating, and she could focus on her own college studies. Margaret had her heart set on attending Wellesley College in Massachusetts, the college her mother had attended.

A Change in Plans

Margaret's studies had not met the language requirements for acceptance at Wellesley. The Meads were now living in New Hope, Pennsylvania, and the Holmquist School for Girls had just opened. There, Margaret took the final courses that would make her eligible for entry to Wellesley College.

Ahead of Her Time

Margaret Mead was ahead of her time—from the way she was raised as a child to her thoughts and opinions as an adult. Margaret was well aware of this. She wrote:

In some ways my upbringing was well ahead of my time—perhaps as much as two generations ahead. Mother's advanced ideas, the way in which all children in our home were treated as persons, the kinds of books I read—ranging from the children's books of my grandmother's generation to the most modern plays that my mother sent for to read with a group of friends—and the way all I read was placed in historical perspective, and above all, the continuous running commentary by my family on schools, on education, on the way teachers were treated by the community . . . all these things represented an extraordinary sophistication and a view of children that was rare in my childhood.[5]

As an anthropologist, Margaret Mead was known for her avant-garde ideas. When she gave a lecture at Stanford University, an audience member was overheard saying, "Whether we like it or not, we'd better pay attention to her. She's not always easy to take, but her thinking is at least fifty years ahead of the rest of us."[6]

Bible School

During the summer, before her college days, Margaret worked as a principal of a Bible school. She wrote, "That summer I really learned about the possibilities of twelve-year-old boys, all of whom seemed determined to catch me out. Later in the field, I was to find twelve-year-old boys my principal resource and I decided that museums should be designed for boys of this age, who were at the height of their intellectual curiosity and skepticism."[7]

However, Margaret would not need those extra language classes. Her father was worried about finances and could not afford to send her to Wellesley. He tried to talk Margaret out of going to college altogether. Her mother talked him into allowing Margaret to attend DePauw University in Indiana. This was Edward's alma mater and was much less costly than Wellesley.

At age 17, Margaret was looking forward to finally going to a school with students who were as intellectual and curious as she was.

Margaret Mead and Luther Cressman, circa 1917

Mead studied anthropology at Barnard College,
a part of Columbia University.

THE COLLEGE YEARS

The fact that Margaret was not going to the college of her choice did not dampen her enthusiasm for the coming year. She looked forward to meeting intellectual students and learning from challenging and interesting professors.

DePauw University

Margaret arrived at the DePauw campus in the fall of 1919. Many surprises awaited Margaret at DePauw. For one, all the school activities were centered on sororities and fraternities. For the most part, the student body was not as interested in intellectual pursuits as in status. A student who was not accepted into a fraternity or sorority was an outcast.

Margaret walked into her first sorority party, proudly wearing her "prairie" dress. Before leaving for the Midwest and DePauw, Margaret had put together a wardrobe for herself. She created a formal dress that represented a prairie with blooming flowers. She never was known for her fashion sense, and this dress was disastrously out of style.

Margaret realized immediately that she did not fit in. No one spoke to her. Margaret was confused by the sorority world and immediately recognized that she was not at all like the other girls. "My unusual clothing was not all that was held against me," Margaret Mead later wrote. "There was my room with its carefully planned color scheme, my books and pictures, and, above all, my tea set. And I did not chew gum. Then, as if these things were not enough, there was my accent."[1]

Margaret had always looked for a best friend in every school she had attended, and it was no different at DePauw. Katherine Rothenberger had transferred to DePauw as a sophomore. She, too, did not belong to a sorority. Margaret and Katherine began a friendship that would last a lifetime. Katherine described Margaret Mead at DePauw as being,

[S]weet and bright and quick, but so lonely, so lost, and she was different. She appeared to know nothing of the Middle West, and although some of her clothes were striking, made of handkerchief linen and that sort of thing, she didn't fit in. But I could tell there was a lot there that other people weren't seeing. [3]

Margaret redeemed herself somewhat by campaigning for Katherine, who was running for vice president of the student body. She was a bit sneaky in her campaign and worked the sororities against each other. Katherine won and became the first female vice president at DePauw. The sororities were beginning to think twice about accepting

Margaret, not so much because they wanted her, but because they did not want her working against them.

After a year at DePauw, it was clear that it was not the right college for Margaret. Wellesley was still too expensive, but Margaret was able to talk her father into letting her go to Barnard College in New York. Luther was in New York as well—an added benefit.

BARNARD COLLEGE

Margaret began her studies at Barnard College in 1920. She found New York City and Barnard to be the intellectually stimulating environment she had hoped for and expected from college. She lived in an apartment with several other young women who also attended Barnard. One of Margaret's favorite pastimes was debating, and there was plenty of debate in her apartment. Margaret and her roommates were intelligent and unique women. They read and wrote poetry, they attended plays and discussed them well into the night, and they embraced the new flapper era.

A NEW ERA

Flappers were women who were spirited, reckless, and rebellious. They wore their hair sleek, often

Barnard College,
Columbia University,
New York City.
March 11,1925.
Dear Grandma,
    Please forgive the formal heading.
I had almost written an elaborate superscript-
ion also.You see in the past week I have
written about forty letters to secretaies of
trade unions and such-like bodies,and formal-
ity itches at my fingers ends.

    Louise and I have just gotten back
from hearing Borah speak on the release of
the Political Prisoners.He is a very delightful speaker,beginning quietly with many
pauses between words and finishing up with
traditional vigour and oratory.A squarely
built man,with thick straight hair,parted in
the middle and cut off squarely just above
his low collar,wearing heavily rimmed eye
glasses that dangle dangerously around his

Mead kept in touch with her grandmother after leaving home.

bobbed, or cut short. They hid their femininity behind shapeless dresses, yet they showed it off by wearing makeup and even applying it in public. Although many of her roommates looked, dressed, and acted like flappers, Margaret did not—except for her bobbed hair. Margaret stayed on the sidelines, mostly because she already was engaged, but she took pleasure in setting up her girlfriends with Luther's classmates.

Her long engagement to Luther allowed Margaret to focus on her friendships with women. Her engagement "was affirming but not demanding. It not only proved to the world that she was a female desired by a male, but, perhaps more important, it 'gave me time,' as she said, 'for deep, creative friendships with women.'"[4]

Margaret and her boisterous and intelligent roommates stood out on campus. When one of the roommates was late to a drama class, the teacher, Minor W. Latham, said, "You girls who sit up all night readin' poetry come to class lookin' like Ash Can Cats!"[5] The name stuck.

At the end of her first year at Barnard, Margaret suffered from severe muscle pains in her right arm and lost strength in her hand. The pain was so extreme that she wore a sling, learned to write with her left hand, and took her exams orally. The diagnosis was neuritis, an inflammation of the nerves. This and other pains plagued Margaret throughout her life.

THE SWITCH TO ANTHROPOLOGY

Margaret's first choice for a major was English. She had always loved literature and had been writing poetry since she was a child. One of her best friends at Barnard, and a member of the Ash Can Cats,

was the soon-to-be-famous poet Léonie Adams.
However, Margaret felt she could not excel in
English. She decided to concentrate on what was
most comfortable—the social sciences. She chose to
major in psychology.

In her senior year, Margaret enrolled in an
anthropology class taught by Franz Boas. This was a
life-changing decision—not only professionally, but
personally as well. Franz Boas's teaching assistant
was the shy and quiet Ruth Benedict. Although she
was 15 years older than Margaret, the two of them
became close friends.

Franz Boas's lectures were formal, and he had
a stern look about him. Ruth Benedict softened
and humanized these lectures. Despite her retiring
manner, Benedict's enthusiasm
for anthropology attracted many
students to this field of study.

Margaret graduated from
Barnard with a bachelor's degree
in psychology in 1923. By the
following spring, Margaret was
working on her master's degree in
psychology, but she was considering
the field of anthropology.

"It wasn't until I got to
Franz Boas that I really
had a teacher who elic-
ited my total respect, so
that I felt he could give
me the ground under my
feet."[6]

—Margaret Mead

Her mind was made up after Benedict told her, "Professor Boas and I have nothing to offer but an opportunity to do work that matters."[7]

Getting Married

Almost six years after their engagement, Margaret and Luther Cressman were married on September 3, 1923. Margaret decided to keep her name, Mead, rather than take the name of Cressman. This was a bold choice in 1923, but she reasoned that she was going to be famous one day. When that day came, Margaret wanted to be known

Ruth Fulton Benedict

Ruth Fulton Benedict was born on June 5, 1887. She played a large role in forming modern cultural anthropology. Some of her most important work was based on her studies of American Indian peoples and the Japanese, during which she developed her theory of culture and personality. Two of her books, *Patterns of Culture* (published in 1934) and *The Chrysanthemum and the Sword* (published in 1946), were best sellers. With these books, Benedict hoped to change the current racist ideas that were based on heredity and environment. Ruth Benedict was also an avid poet and published her works under the pseudonym Anne Singleton.

Benedict joined the Columbia University faculty in 1923, where she taught and influenced young anthropologists, including Margaret Mead. She was the first woman appointed to a full-time faculty position at Columbia in 1931. She and Franz Boas were the only anthropology professors at Columbia. Benedict was awarded many academic honors and was elected president of the American Anthropological Association in 1947. Ruth Fulton Benedict died on September 17, 1948, at the age of 61 in New York City.

by her last name, not her husband's. Luther agreed to this.

Not long after their wedding, Margaret's vision of herself as a minister's wife was fading. Luther had lost interest in the ministry and turned his attention to sociology. The young couple moved into a small apartment in New York City and continued their lives as students.

Columbia had four graduate students in anthropology in 1924. Boas wanted to oversee his students' placement in the field so that each study would benefit anthropology to the greatest extent. Margaret wanted to start her fieldwork as soon as possible. Once Samoa was selected, she needed to find a fellowship to help finance her trip. The Board of the National Research Council offered her a $150-a-month fellowship.

Margaret and Luther discussed the possibility of Luther going to Samoa with her, but they decided he would look for a fellowship to pursue in his own course of study. He was offered a European travel fellowship and would work in Europe while Margaret was in Samoa. In the fall of 1925, Luther left for Europe and Margaret started her journey to Samoa.

Ruth Benedict was one of Margaret Mead's good friends and colleagues.

Mead sitting between two Samoan girls in 1926

SAMOA

argaret Mead chose to go into anthropology partly because of concerns voiced by Professor Boas and Professor Benedict. More and more, distant societies were exposed to the modern world. Previously isolated peoples were putting aside their traditional cultures and histories for more alluring modern ways. Boas and Benedict feared that soon it would be too late to find societies to study that were untouched by the modern world, and the opportunity to learn more about human nature would be lost. Mead also saw the potential to add useful information to existing scientific knowledge of humanity, something her father held very dear.

Preparing for her first fieldwork in Samoa, Mead packed six cotton dresses. Although she would have preferred silk, she had heard that silk would rot in the tropics with temperatures ranging from 80 degrees to 90 degrees Fahrenheit (26.7° to 32.2°C) and humidity levels to match. Rain showers up to five times a day were a normal event in Samoa. Mead also packed a small safe for money, papers, a small camera, and a portable typewriter.

On her way to Samoa, Mead stopped in Honolulu, Hawaii, for two weeks. She stayed with May

Changing the Language of Anthropology

In Mead's day, anthropologists used terms such as "primitive" and "advanced" to describe a culture or society. These terms were used because most anthropologists believed that cultures progress through a series of developmental stages: primitive, savage, barbaric, and civilized.

Modern anthropologists no longer accept this theory. Today, anthropologists use terms such as "simple," "complex," "traditional," and "nonliterate" to describe the cultures and societies they are studying.

Dillingham Freer, one of her mother's college friends. An influential woman, Freer helped Mead with various details of her trip. While in Honolulu, arrangements were made for Mead to visit two children who were part Samoan. And for a week, Mead took lessons in Marquesan, a language related to Samoan.

The First Weeks

Mead finally arrived in Pago Pago. She spent a lonely and dismal six weeks with nothing to do but learn the local language. Then it was off to Vaitogi. The mother of the part–Samoan children Mead had

---

A Letter from Professor Boas

Before Mead left for Samoa, Franz Boas wrote her a letter to clarify the purpose of her fieldwork. He was clearly interested in the variations or similarities in behaviors of adolescents in simpler societies and those in Western society of the mid-1920s. In this letter he wrote:

One question that interests me very much is how the young girls react to the restraints of custom. We find very often among ourselves during the period of adolescence a strong rebellious spirit that may be expressed in sullenness or in sudden outbursts. In other individuals there is a weak submission which is accompanied, however, by a suppressed rebellion that may make itself felt in peculiar ways, perhaps in a desire for solitude which is really an expression of desire for freedom, or otherwise in forced participation in social affairs in order to drown the mental troubles. I am not at all clear in my mind in how far similar conditions may occur in primitive society and in how far the desire for independence may be simply due to our modern conditions and to a more strongly developed individualism.[1]

met in Honolulu had arranged for her to stay with a chief and his family. This gave Mead the opportunity to practice her language skills and learn about Samoan custom. She wrote, "Speaking on one's feet within the house is still an unforgivable breech of etiquette, and the visitor must learn to sit cross-legged for hours without murmuring."[2] Mead also learned to give long speeches and eat first, before the villagers ate, because she was the guest.

Although her stay was short, Mead and the chief's family became close. The family admired her ability to speak their language and learn their customs. Mead was grateful for their hospitality and all that they had taught her about Samoan life. But it was time to go to Tau, where she would conduct her fieldwork.

Tau was the only island that fit all of Mead's criteria: It was still mostly untouched by the modern world, and it had enough adolescent girls for her study. Plus, she would be able to live with Americans—a perfect situation.

In some ways, Mead felt much like an adolescent when she did her

Doubts

Years after her work in Samoa, some people questioned Mead's ability to speak Samoan. She did not have a reputation for learning languages easily. Other anthropologists and people who did know how to speak the Samoan language questioned whether six weeks was long enough for Mead to have a grasp on the language.

fieldwork in Samoa. She weighed approximately 100 pounds (45.4 kg) and barely topped five feet, three inches (1.7 m) in height. Similar to adolescents in the United States, Mead was insecure about the work she was doing. She wrote,

> *I had no idea whether I was using the right methods. What were the right methods? There were no precedents to fall back on. I wrote to Professor Boas just before I left for Pago Pago, outlining my plans. His reassuring answer arrived after I had finished my work on Tau and was ready to leave![3]*

LIFE IN TAU

In Tau, Mead's base of operations and the place she called home was the porch of the clinic. This arrangement gave Mead some freedom she would not otherwise have had. Mead described her living arrangements in Tau:

> *Living in the dispensary, I could do things that otherwise would have been wholly inappropriate. The adolescent girls, and later the smaller girls whom I found I had also to study, came and filled my screen-room day after day and night after night. Later I borrowed a schoolhouse to give "examinations," and under that heading I was able to give a few simple tests and interview each girl alone. . . . Gradually I built up a*

Mead's room in Samoa

census of the whole village and worked out the background of each of the girls I was studying. . . . I learned a great deal of ethnology, but I never had any political participation in village life.[4]

Professor Boas had warned Mead that much of her time, especially at first, would be spent just getting to know the adolescent girls. He thought she might feel as though all she was doing was sitting around and wasting time. He feared the work of an anthropologist might bore Mead. But the ever-active Mead fell into step with the calm and quietness of Tau and the routine of observation.

Mead loved to read, but she had no books or journals with her in Samoa. She did find an alternative to reading books: She read letters. Letters were brought to Mead by boat every few weeks. She often received 70 to 80 letters from her family, friends, and colleagues. The news would be weeks late, but the letters kept her connected to the important people in her life. Being so far away from home and the familiar made her feel lonely and out of touch. Mead wrote,

> It is frustrated gentleness that is so hard to bear when one is working for long months alone in the field. Some fieldworkers adopt a dog or a kitten; I much prefer babies.[5]

"Well"

On New Year's Day 1926, Tau was hit by a huge storm. The wind tossed coconuts, sand, and parts of homes through the air. Nearly every house was destroyed. But the Holts's house, where Mead had found refuge, remained standing. Word of the storm got back to the United States, but no one knew if Mead had survived. Ruth Benedict finally received a one-word cable from Mead on January 12. It read "Well." Benedict forwarded the good news to Mead's family.

RETURNING HOME

After nine months in Samoa, Mead had finished her research. Mead's trip had been successful. She had completed her fieldwork unaided, creating methods to quantify her tests and observations. Her conclusions would please her mentor, Franz Boas, very much. Mead's work in Samoa confirmed that one's culture was more of a factor in determining gender roles and attitudes among adolescent girls than one's biology. It was now time to return home.

From Pago Pago, it was a six-week trip by ship to Europe, where she was to meet Luther. She also planned on meeting her college roommate, Louise Rosenblatt, and Ruth Benedict in Paris, France. The first leg of her trip brought her to Sydney, Australia, where she spent some time with Luther's Australian relatives. The second leg of the trip was postponed for a few days. Most of the passengers stayed on shore, but a few, including Mead, boarded the ship. Mead planned to spend this time organizing her field notes. But she happened to cross paths with a young psychologist from New Zealand named Reo Fortune.

Makelita

The Samoans liked Mead so much they nicknamed her Makelita after one of their dead queens.

On the surface, it appeared that Reo Fortune and Margaret Mead had little in common. Fortune had grown up in a fairly isolated area of New Zealand and had not been exposed to art and culture. What he did have in common with Mead was books. Academics and learning were important to Reo. He was on his way to Cambridge University in the United Kingdom. He had won a two-year fellowship to Cambridge for an essay he had written about dreams.

Reo was quite different from Mead's husband. Luther was relaxed and understanding of nearly any situation. Reo was driven, ambitious, and prone to jealousy. Mead and Reo were involved in an intense conversation when the ship docked in Europe. As the passengers disembarked from the ship, Mead and Reo continued to talk. When they realized the ship had docked, they, too, disembarked. This was one of the rare moments in her life that Mead immediately regretted and wished she could take back. Anxiously waiting for her on the deserted shore was her husband, Luther. What did he think when he saw his wife leave the ship with a young, handsome man?

One of Mead's field notebooks from Samoa

Margaret Mead and Reo Fortune in Pere Village, Manus, 1928

THE ADMIRALTY ISLANDS

fter sightseeing in Europe with Luther and some college friends, Mead returned to New York in 1926. Luther had found an apartment for them, and Mead began her first job as the assistant curator of ethnology at the American Museum of Natural History. This was the perfect job for Mead because it gave her the opportunity to lecture and write. During this time, she wrote *Coming of Age in Samoa*. She also wrote her doctoral thesis, *An Inquiry into the Question of Cultural Stability in Polynesia*, for the scholarly audience. Meanwhile, she and Reo Fortune kept in touch with each other.

After writing additional chapters requested by her publisher, *Coming of Age in Samoa* was accepted for publication. Mead wrote this book so that anthropology in general and her specific work on adolescence could be brought to America's attention. She related what she had learned in Samoa, that culture and not biology determined behavior, with the hope of making American lives better. But she did not want to stop there. Mead began thinking about writing for magazines so she could reach more people. Many of her colleagues, though, warned her that writing for the general public could harm her career. They worried she would not be taken seriously as a scholar.

Controversy

Some of the issues raised in *Coming of Age in Samoa* would be hotly discussed and argued over for more than half a century, well after Mead's death. One such issue was her questioning the need for the nuclear family. Mead's preference was for a family community made up of several adult women and men who share in the raising of their children.

Separate Goals

When Margaret and Luther married, they had similar goals for their lives together. They wanted to work with people through their involvement with the church, and they planned on having six children. Now, neither one of them was interested in pursuing work within a church. And Margaret discovered that she could not have children. The vision of their lives together had changed drastically. Margaret and Luther were now pursuing individual and separate goals. The following summer, in 1928, her marriage to Luther came to an end.

Margaret and Luther remained on friendly terms, though their friends thought Margaret was cruel by planning her wedding to Reo while still spending time with Luther. No one but Margaret knew that Luther had a new relationship and was planning to remarry as well.

A New Science

During the 1920s, psychoanalysis had been introduced by Sigmund Freud and created a lot of interest among scholarly Americans. Mead and her circle of friends and colleagues were among those intrigued with this new science.

Freud, among other scientists, believed that the minds of adults in traditional, isolated societies had much in common with those of American children. Mead became so interested in this topic that she wanted to make it the subject of her next study. She applied for and received a social science research fellowship to study the thinking processes of children under five years of age in the Admiralty Islands.

Details

Junius Bird, curator of South American Archeology at the American Museum of Natural History, said of Mead, "What made her a legend so early was the way she emphasized details of a native culture that nobody else would have noticed."[1]

Mead selected the Admiralty Islands on the recommendation of a prominent British anthropologist, Alfred Reginald Radcliffe-Brown. Reo Fortune could join her and continue his study of "primitive" religion. To prepare for the fieldwork, Mead created and assembled tests and toys that would help her conduct her research. Before Mead left New York in 1928, she saw a prepublication version of *Coming of Age in Samoa*. It would be published while she was deep into her fieldwork in the Admiralty Islands.

On her way to the Admiralty Islands, Mead met Fortune in Auckland, New Zealand. As soon as the boat docked, he informed her that they would be married that day. They had difficulty finding a ring small enough to fit Margaret's tiny finger, but they finally found someone who could alter a ring to size.

MANUS

In 1928, Mead and Fortune set off for Manus in the Admiralty Islands. They had selected the village of Pere as their focus. They arrived at midnight, after a long day of travel. Mead wrote, "The dome-shaped houses stood high on piles in the shallow lagoon amid tiny islands of palm trees. The mainland—Manus— was a dark shadow in the distance."[3]

Mead and her new husband stayed in homes that were typical of the villages they studied. In Pere, the homes were

---

Drawings

As part of her research, Mead asked the children of Pere to draw pictures for her. At that time, the belief in the supernatural was considered a stage of development in childhood that was experienced by children of all cultures. The people of Manus believed in the supernatural. But instead of drawing pictures of fantastical, supernatural subjects, the children drew realistic pictures of their everyday life. Mead also gave the children inkblot tests. They were asked to describe the picture they saw in a splatter of ink. Again, they described the common things around them. From her data, Mead reached the conclusion that the children of Pere did not think supernaturally. She wrote, "What is considered childlike in thought varies according to the emphases of the culture."[2]

Mead collected approximately 35,000 drawings by the children of Pere. These findings were published in 1932 as an article titled "An Investigation into the Thought of Primitive Children with Special Reference to Animism."

---

built high over the water. To enter a home, one had to climb a ladder. The possibility of falling into the water was constant, so water safety was one of the first skills taught to the children of Pere.

Apparently, children were not the only ones who had to worry about safety in this village. One day, as Mead climbed the ladder to her home in Pere, it fell apart and she broke her ankle. The people in Manus set her bone and built crutches for her.

PUBLICATIONS

When Mead and Fortune returned to New York in September 1929, their friends greeted them with the news of Mead's newfound fame. Her book, *Coming of Age in Samoa*, had become a best seller. It was clear that in this marriage and in their professions, Fortune would take a backseat to Mead.

Margaret Mead and Reo Fortune spent the following two years in New York City. Mead resumed her position at the American Museum of Natural History. The country entered the Great Depression.

Broken Ankle

Mead broke her ankle three times in her life. The first time, a New York City taxi sideswiped her in 1924. The second time, she fell off the ladder in Pere. The final time was in 1960. She then began using what she called a shepherd's staff to help her walk. This tall, forked walking stick became one of her trademarks.

Mead's salary at the museum was reduced, but she did have her job. Mead also received her PhD in anthropology from Columbia University. During this period, Mead wrote about her research. For a general audience, Mead wrote *Growing Up in New Guinea* in 1930, which she dedicated to Reo Fortune. She later wrote a technical paper entitled "Kinship in the Admiralty Islands." Both were reports of her findings in Manus.

In *Growing Up in New Guinea*, Mead explained that adults in traditional, nonliterate societies were not like American children, as some had believed. She also established that the stages of human developmental varied among different cultures. Mead became the first anthropologist to look at human development along cross-cultural lines.

Criticisms

Franz Boas's first PhD student, Alfred Kroeber, criticized Mead for not having enough ethnological data to support her conclusions. But he could not help but show his admiration as well. He said, "She had an aesthetic gift for conceptualization 'approaching genius.'"[4]

TRAVELS IN NEW GUINEA

In December 1931, Mead and Fortune were off again to New Guinea. But this time they went to the village of Alitoa to study people speaking Arapesh languages. Mead was studying the ways culture

Mead in Alitoa Village, Arapesh, 1932

shaped the behavior of males and females. The trails to the village were extremely steep. Mead's weak ankle dictated that once she arrived, she would have to stay until it was time to leave for good. She felt trapped, especially since Fortune could come and go as he pleased. Mead and Fortune left the Arapesh in August 1932, after seven and a half months of research. With their supplies replenished, they traveled up the Sepik River to find another site. They stayed on the lower portion of the river so they would not interfere with their colleague Gregory Bateson's work in the middle Sepik. Fortune and Mead studied the Mundugumor people.

This was a miserable time. There were so many mosquitoes that Mead wore Fortune's pajama bottoms under her dress for protection. Not surprisingly, Mead fought a fever, probably malaria, much of the time. And it was difficult to like the Mundugumor people. Mead wrote,

> *Most difficult of all for me to bear was the Mundugumor attitude toward children. Women wanted sons and men wanted daughters, and babies of the wrong sex were tossed into the river, still alive, wrapped in a bark sheath.*[5]

While some of the ways of the Mundugumor repelled Fortune, they also fascinated him. They brought out parts of his personality that were completely unfamiliar to Mead. At that time, Mead and Fortune were not getting along well. After only three months, they decided to leave.

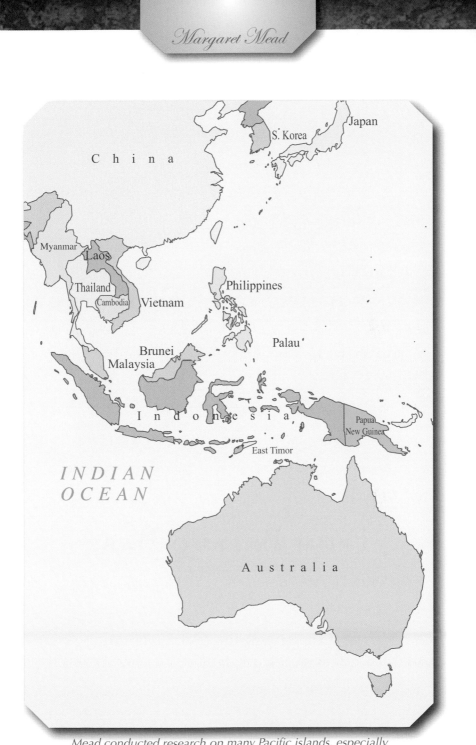

*Mead conducted research on many Pacific islands, especially
New Guinea and the more isolated surrounding islands.*

Gregory Bateson, Margaret Mead, and Reo Fortune, July 1933

FROM BALI TO BABY

A fter leaving the Mundugumor, Mead and Fortune stopped at the Iatmul village, where Gregory Bateson was doing his fieldwork in 1933. Bateson had been working alone for so long that he was eager for academic conversation. He and Fortune stayed up all night talking.

Two days after Christmas, the three anthropologists traveled up the Sepik River to visit the Washkuk tribe, whom Fortune and Mead were considering for their next study. But the tribe begged them not to stay because taking care of them would be a great inconvenience. The three agreed, though they did stay overnight. The Washkuk expected a raid from another tribe, so Fortune and Bateson took turns keeping watch. Mead stayed up and spent the night talking with Bateson.

TCHAMBULI

In the spring of 1933, Bateson introduced Mead and Fortune to the Tchambuli, who lived on the Sepik River as well. Mead wrote,

> *Tchambuli was providing a kind of pattern—in fact, the missing piece—that made possible a new interpretation of what we already knew. Very often it is only this kind of comparison of different cultures that reveals what the dimensions of a problem actually are, and so enables one to restate the problem in new terms. Contrast through comparison is necessary to complete a picture.*[1]

During this time, Bateson continued his research on the Iatmul only a few miles away. Periodically, the three anthropologists visited and shared notes. They began talking about the possibility of people being born with certain temperaments. By comparing the cultures they had studied, Mead, Fortune, and Bateson searched for relationships among temperament, gender, and culturally expected behavior. They also examined the cultures of their respective

The Beauty of Tchambuli

In her book *Sex and Temperament in Three Primitive Societies*, Mead described Aibom Lake, on which the Tchambuli lived, in language as beautiful as the place itself. With Mead's poetic prose, it is no wonder her books were admired outside of academic circles.

The water of the lake is so coloured with dark peat-brown vegetable matter that it looks black on the surface, and when no wind stirs it, resembles black enamel. On this polished surface, in still times the leaves of thousands of pink and white lotuses and a smaller deep-blue water-lily are spread, and among the flowers, in the early morning, the white osprey and the blue heron stand in great numbers, completing the decorative effect, which displays almost too studied a pattern to seem completely real. When the wind blows and ruffles the black surface to a cold blue, the lotus-leaves that lay so inert and thick upon the enamel surface are ruffled, and lifting lightly along their stems, show themselves to be not a green monotone, but a variable rose and silver-green, and of a delicate and pliant thinness. The small sharp hills that edge the lake gather clouds upon their summits which resemble snow and accentuate their steep rise from the fen-land level.[2]

countries—the United States, New Zealand, and England. This gave them a newfound understanding of each other. They wondered if they could use temperaments to classify people and cultures.

One revelation that came from these discussions was that every society has its deviants, people who do not represent the norm. Mead revealed:

> Both Gregory and I felt that we were, to some extent, deviants, each within our own culture. Many of the forms of aggressive male behavior that were standardized in English culture did not appeal to him. My own interest in children did not fit the stereotype of the American career woman. . . . It was exciting to strip off the layers of culturally attributed expected behavior and to feel that one knew at last who one was.[3]

Fortune did not experience the same realization as Bateson and Mead. Nevertheless, Mead and Fortune cabled Franz Boas to inform him that they had made an incredible discovery.

Another realization was that Mead and Bateson fell in love. In the summer of 1933, the trio returned to Australia and then

Other Anthropologists

Margaret Mead repeated a comment Gregory Bateson once made about her, "Anthropologists who had read my work but did not know me tended to doubt my conclusions because they could not allow for the speed with which I worked."[4]

continued on their separate ways. Bateson journeyed home to Cambridge, Fortune also went to England, and Mead returned to New York. Mead and Fortune would not see each other again until after their divorce in 1935.

Sex and Temperament in Three Primitive Societies, Mead's book about her work with the Arapesh, the Mundugumor, and the Tchambuli was published in the spring of 1935. Mead and Bateson were married in Singapore and soon began their fieldwork in Bali in 1936.

The Importance of Pictures

Bali was a beautiful island with much music and ritual. Mead and Bateson chose the village of Bajoeng Gede as their base of operation, although they would travel to other parts of Bali.

One day while Mead was taking notes, Bateson shot 60 photographs and 200 feet (61 m) of film. This was a significant moment for the couple. They realized how photography could help them document sequences of events. They invested the little money they had in additional film. Mead recognized that this new methodology was a more accurate and more efficient means of

Mead and Bateson documented their research
with photographs in Bajoeng Gede, Bali.

documentation. She used film to study how people
communicated through gestures. Mead and Bateson
had originally planned on taking approximately
2,000 photographs while in Bali but ended up with
25,000. They also shot 22,000 feet (6,700 m) of
film.

This new form of anthropological documentation was revolutionary and its value was recognized. Thirty-five years later, at a symposium of the American Anthropological Association in 1971, Bateson's 1936 films were held up as the model of photographic documentation.

MOTHERHOOD

Given her role models, Mead had expected to be both a career woman and a mother. When she married her first husband, she had planned on having six children. But their plans changed when a doctor told her that she would not be able to have children. Mead never gave up the desire to be a mother.

Her profession gave her ample opportunity to interact with children of all ages, which she greatly enjoyed—except when it came to the Mundugumor people. This aggressive society seemed to reject children. It was through her experience with these people that Mead was determined to have a baby regardless of how many miscarriages she would have to suffer.

Mead and Bateson left Bali in 1938, stopping for six months in Iatmul to make some comparative studies. By that time, Mead had experienced a number of miscarriages and false alarms. In 1939, as England was gearing up for World War II, Mead learned she was pregnant. Mead wrote,

> *And so it came about, that at thirty-eight, after many years of experience as a student of child development and of childbirth in remote villages . . . I was to share in the wartime experience of young wives all around the world.[5]*

As a soldier, Bateson had to fight in the war. Mead's major focus at this time was to find a doctor who would allow her to raise her baby her own way. She wanted to breast-feed her baby on demand, not according to a schedule, which is what doctors recommended at that time. She also wanted to keep her baby with her in the hospital. After much searching, she chose Dr. Benjamin Spock for her child's pediatrician.

On December 8, 1939, Mary Catherine Bateson was born. Bateson was still overseas, so Mead

Dr. Benjamin Spock

Dr. Spock, Mead's pediatrician, became as popular in his field as Mead was in hers. In 1946, he wrote *The Common Sense Book of Baby and Child Care*. In it, he challenged the thinking of the day by recommending that parents trust their own judgment regarding their children rather than follow strict rules. Spock became so popular that his book could be found in nearly every family household in America.

moved back into her parents' house. Six weeks later, Bateson returned and met his daughter for the first time. In the Mead family tradition, detailed notes were lovingly kept of Catherine's early development.

Mead was influenced by the various cultures she had studied as well as her own childhood. She wanted to raise her child with an extended family. In the summer, the Batesons lived in New Hampshire in the communal household of friend and colleague Larry Frank. Other occupants of the house were Bateson's two teenage goddaughters, a nanny, her teenage daughter, and Frank's family, which included his wife and five children.

This communal living arrangement worked well for Mead. In a way, Catherine had many mothers. As Mead frequently went on trips to lecture or attend meetings, she never had to worry about Catherine; someone trustworthy was always there to care for her.

World Issues

During World War II, Bateson and Mead wanted to do what they could as social scientists to help the United States. Bateson and other anthropologists were asked to serve as cultural experts to aid the Allies with research to gain insights into their enemies. Mead followed in her mother's footsteps. Her mother was a Progressive who believed that the social sciences could solve the problems of society.

Mead's focus shifted from working with distant cultures to analyzing "complex cultures," such as the United States. Interested in global interdependence, Mead became more involved in international organizations that worked on worldwide human issues.

In 1943, Mead accepted the position of executive secretary for the National Research Council's Committee on Food Habits, in Washington DC. The committee looked at anthropological methods to solve problems of food preparation and distribution in countries during wartime. When people were denied certain kinds of food, their stress increased during what was already a stressful

Anthropology during World War II

World War II prompted anthropologists to examine complex societies, such as Japan, by applying the techniques they had perfected in small villages. These anthropologists did not travel to faraway places to conduct their studies. Rather, they studied cultures from afar by pulling together information from publications, interviews with immigrants, and films. Their goals were to guide governmental and military policies, aid cooperation among wartime allies, and help plan for the days after the war.

situation. They focused on determining the foods that were "must-haves" for people from varying cultural backgrounds. They found that they could maintain morale by ensuring people had access to the food that was important to them. ⌐

Mead conducts an interview on United Nations Radio in 1952.

Chapter 9

Mead working at the American Museum of Natural History

GRANDMOTHER OF THE GLOBAL VILLAGE

*I*n the 1940s, Margaret Mead turned her attention from simpler societies to complex cultures such as the United States, England, and Germany. She was interested in using the principles of anthropology to address social issues such as education and world hunger. She became involved with many organizations that promoted international research. In 1944, she founded the Institute for Intercultural Studies to advance

> *knowledge of the various peoples and nations of the world, with special attention to those peoples and those aspects of their life which are likely to affect intercultural and international relations.*[1]

Mead continued to travel and lecture all over the world. She usually went without Bateson, who was busy with his own career and travels. She was lonely without her husband and missed him during these times. Wherever she went, she made sure her schedule was packed, possibly to combat that loneliness. If she were speaking at a symposium, for example, she would also line up lectures at local universities and visit friends or family in the area—usually with very little notice. She also tried to get home as often as she could to spend time with her daughter.

Bringing Ideas Together

Mead was willing to talk about nearly any subject, whether or not she had the qualifications. One of her talents was tying together vastly diverse topics. A reporter attending one of Mead's lectures at the American Museum of Natural History remarked on how she "managed to discuss museums, stones, stuffed birds, cave paintings, Cro-Magnon man, children, parents, grandparents, dinosaurs, whales, the possibility of life in outer space, education, the youth revolution of the 1960s, the oneness of the human species, pollution, evolution, growing up in New Guinea, relations between the sexes, communes and the fragmentation of communities."[2]

New Technology

August 6, 1945, marked the beginning of the nuclear age when the United States dropped an atomic bomb on Hiroshima, Japan. The bomb caused unbelievable destruction. The world would never be the same. For Mead, the bombing marked a period of growing interest in how science and new technology affected people and societies. She spent the rest of her life looking for ways people could adjust to and thrive in a new world of growing technological complexity.

Through most of her life, Mead had been interested in cultural stability and change. Now new technologies increased the pace of change in societies. Mead wanted to look at how this affected the relationship between one generation and the next. She once said,

> *I have seen what few people have ever seen, people who have moved from the Stone Age into the present in 30 years—kids who say, "My father was a cannibal, but I am going to be a doctor!"*[3]

In the 1950s, Margaret Mead and her colleague and friend, Rhoda Métraux, began studying how American students viewed scientists. In 1957, when the Soviet satellite *Sputnik* was launched, their study included children's drawings of the satellite. Later, Mead returned to Bali and spoke to high school boys about the recent launch, and she collected their drawings of *Sputnik*. She later noted,

> *At this moment in history, we have virtually the whole of man's life spread out before us—people who are living as they may have lived for the past 30,000 years and astronauts who are beginning to live as we will live tomorrow.*[4]

In the Spotlight

With Bateson and Mead spending so much time apart, it was not surprising that Bateson moved out on his own. In her prior relationships, Mead was the one who left. This separation upset her a great deal. They divorced in October 1950.

Mead became even more in demand by the public. She and Rhoda Métraux wrote a monthly

Public Persona

Melvin Maddocks described Mead's controversial public persona: "Should marriage vows cover more than five years? Must infants be so swaddled? Need adolescents feel guilt? Before television cameras, on hundreds of lecture platforms, in thousands of lines of print, Margaret Mead emphatically doubted it. Flouncing her cape, thumping her cherry-wood walking stick and shouting, 'Fiddlesticks!' (her battle cry against cant), she became one of those native oracles, full of cranky common sense and hearty exhortation."[5]

column in the women's magazine *Redbook* for 17 years, from 1961 to 1978. Mead also gave radio and television interviews. She was broadcast over the airwaves so frequently that she had to join the American Federation of Radio and Television Artists—the only anthropologist required to join this union of professional entertainers. As she became more visible, though, she also became more controversial.

Fame

Margaret Mead's critics were far outnumbered by her fans. As acclaimed cultural anthropologist Wilton S. Dillon wrote, "The process by which a young woman, with travel money from her professor father, could set sail from Morningside Heights to Samoa with her notebooks and camera and, nearly 55 years later, without a big bureaucracy or wealth behind her, command the attention of bishops, revolutionaries, bankers, legislators, monarchs, housewives, husbands and children, and the deaf and the blind, to name a few constituencies, is worthy of study by all interested in leadership and how knowledge is brought to bear on human choices."[6]

CONTROVERSY

Along with serving on a vast number of committees, Mead made more and more public appearances. With her strong voice and even stronger opinions, she won many friends and also made many enemies. Some even called her names such as "dirty old lady" or "international busybody."

Along with fame came controversy and criticism of her work. Many critics were scientists who felt that, by writing for the lay reader, she compromised her credibility. Others said that she did not always use scientific methods and made too many inferences. Derek Freeman, an anthropologist from Australia, was perhaps Mead's most vocal critic. Freeman spent much of his time trying to disprove Mead's work. His book, *Margaret Mead and Samoa: The Making and Unmaking of an Anthropological Myth*, detailed the errors he believed Mead had made that were described in her first book, *Coming of Age in Samoa*. Freeman's book created an uproar among anthropologists and laypeople. Eventually, the American Anthropological Association (AAA) issued a statement in support of Margaret Mead and her work. Freeman continued to discredit Mead for much of his life. Many people continue to support his view of Mead's work.

THE END

In 1977, friends and colleagues noticed that Mead was losing weight, and, it seemed, some of her energy and zeal as well.

Despite her age, Mead kept up her grueling schedule of traveling and lecturing. For a long time, she refused to acknowledge that she was not feeling well. Even when she was diagnosed with pancreatic cancer, she would not openly admit to her illness and did not allow it to become public knowledge.

Mead did not really believe she was dying; her willpower, she thought, would get her through this. Only a week before her death she had said,

> They finally found out what's wrong with me. It is cancer, and I want the world to know that. Now that they know what it is, they can start doing something to treat it.[8]

On November 15, 1978, Margaret Mead died. She was buried at Trinity Church in Buckingham, Pennsylvania. Many memorial services followed, some as far away as the Polynesian islands of the South Pacific. After she died, the people of Manus rested seven days in mourning, and then planted a coconut tree in her honor. ⌐

Mead at her office in New York

TIMELINE

1901	1919	1920
Margaret Mead is born on December 16 in Philadelphia, Pennsylvania.	Mead enrolls at DePauw University at Greencastle, Indiana.	Mead transfers to Barnard College at Columbia University, where she meets Franz Boas and Ruth Benedict.

1926	1926	1928
Mead meets Reo Fortune.	Mead is appointed assistant curator of ethnology at the American Museum of Natural History in New York City.	*Coming of Age in Samoa* is published. Mead and Cressman divorce; Mead marries Fortune.

1923

Mead marries Luther Cressman in September and receives her BA from Barnard.

1924

Mead receives her MA in psychology from Columbia University.

1925

Mead leaves to do fieldwork in Samoa.

1928

Mead and Fortune do fieldwork among the Manus tribe of the Admiralty Islands in the West Pacific until 1929.

1929

Fortune and Mead return to New York; Mead receives her PhD in anthropology from Columbia University.

1930

Growing Up in New Guinea is published.

TIMELINE

1931

Mead leaves to do fieldwork with Fortune in New Guinea. They study the Arapesh, Mundugumor, and the Tchambuli.

1935

Sex and Temperament in Three Primitive Societies is published. Mead divorces Fortune and marries Gregory Bateson.

1936

Mead and Bateson do fieldwork in Bali and New Guinea.

1951

Mead serves as vice president of the American Association of Science and of the American Council of Learned Sciences.

1954

Mead becomes adjunct professor of anthropology at Columbia University.

1960

Mead serves as president of the American Anthropological Association. Mead's daughter marries.

1939	1943	1950
Mead and Bateson's daughter, Mary Catherine Bateson, is born on December 8.	Mead serves as executive secretary of the Committee on Food Habits, National Research Council until 1945.	Mead and Bateson divorce.

1961	1964	1978
Mead begins writing a column for *Redbook* with Rhoda Métraux.	Mead is appointed a curator at the American Museum of Natural History.	Margaret Mead dies on November 15.

Essential Facts

Date of Birth
December 16, 1901

Place of Birth
Philadelphia, Pennsylvania

Date of Death
November 15, 1978

Parents
Edward Sherwood Mead and Emily Fogg Mead

Education
DePauw University, Greencastle, Indiana
Barnard College, New York, New York; BA
Columbia University, New York, New York; MA, PhD

Marriages
Luther Cressman (1923–1928)
Reo Fortune (1928–1935)
Gregory Bateson (1935–1950)

Children
Mary Catherine Bateson (b. 1939)

Career Highlights
Mead studied adolescence in cultures that had not been exposed to modern Western influences. She gained national recognition with the publication of *Coming of Age in Samoa*.

Societal Contribution

Mead dispelled certain racist ideas about cultures that had not been introduced to modern Western society. She also provided the anthropological community with evidence that one's culture may have more effect on a person's behavior than one's biology.

Residences

The Meads moved about 60 times during Margaret Mead's childhood. Among her homes: Hammonton, New Jersey; Holicong, Pennsylvania; Philadelphia, Pennsylvania; New York, New York.

Public Conflicts

Mead was criticized by her peers for publishing her work informally for the public in magazines such as *Redbook*. Her methods of collecting data have also been called into question, especially by Derek Freeman.

Private Conflicts

Mead wanted to have a child but had difficulty becoming pregnant. She was married and divorced three times.

Quote

"I have spent most of my life studying the lives of other peoples, faraway peoples, so that Americans might better understand themselves."—*Margaret Mead*

ADDITIONAL RESOURCES

SELECT BIBLIOGRAPHY

Bateson, Mary Catherine. *With a Daughter's Eye*. New York: William Morrow & Company, 1984.

Howard, Jane. *Margaret Mead: A Life*. New York: Simon and Schuster, 1984.

"Margaret Mead: Human Nature and the Power of Culture." Library of Congress. <http://www.loc.gov/exhibits/mead/>.

Mead, Margaret. *Blackberry Winter: My Early Years*. New York: William Morrow & Company, 1972.

Mead, Margaret. *Letters from the Field 1925–1975*. Ed. Nanda Anshen. New York: Harper & Row, Publishers, 1977.

Mead, Margaret. *To Cherish the Life of the World: Selected Letters of Margaret Mead*. Ed. Margaret M. Caffrey and Patricia A. Francis. New York: Basic Books, 2006.

FURTHER READING

Baldwin, James, and Margaret Mead. *A Rap on Race*. New York: Dell Publishing, 1992.

Quinn, Stephen C. *Windows on Nature: The Great Habitat Dioramas of the American Museum of Natural History*. New York: Harry N. Abrams, Inc., 2006.

Swisher, Clarice. *Women of the Roaring Twenties*. Farmington Hills, MI: Gale Group, 2005.

WEB LINKS

To learn more about Margaret Mead, visit ABDO Publishing Company online at **www.abdopublishing.com**. Web sites about Margaret Mead are featured on our Book Links page. These links are routinely monitored and updated to provide the most current information available.

Places to Visit

American Museum of Natural History
Central Park West at Seventy-ninth Street
New York, NY 10024
212-769-5000
www.amnh.org
Margaret Mead worked at the museum's anthropology department
for most of her life. Visit the Hall of Pacific People to see artifacts
from areas in which Mead did her studies.

Home of Margaret Mead
2675 Holicong Road
Holicong, PA 18928
www.visitpa.com/visitpa/tripgenViewMap.pa?transaction=locMap&t
emplate=map&recordId=236951&attractionId=236951&name-
Home+Of+Margaret+Mead
Visit the large 18-room farmhouse in which Margaret Mead spent
much of her childhood.

Margaret Mead Green
Theodore Roosevelt Park
Central Park West, Columbus Avenue, between West Seventy-
seventh and West Eighty-first Streets
New York, NY 10023
212-260-1616
www.nycgovparks.org/sub_your_park/historical_signs/hs_historical_
sign.php?id=7892
In 1979, the northwest portion of Theodore Roosevelt Park was
officially named the Margaret Mead Green as a lasting tribute to
Margaret Mead.

GLOSSARY

animism
> A belief in spirits within natural phenomena such as trees, rocks, and thunder.

anthropology
> The study of human beings and their ancestors.

archeology
> The scientific study of ancient peoples through the excavation of material remains, such as fossils and artifacts, of past human life and activities.

avant-garde
> New or unconventional concepts.

cultural anthropology
> A division of anthropology that deals with all aspects of human culture.

curator
> A person who is in charge of a collection or a department in a museum, library, or zoo.

ethnology
> A form of anthropology that deals chiefly with the comparative and analytical study of cultures.

extended family
> A family that includes more people than just the father, mother, and children living together.

fellowship
> A sum of money paid by a foundation to support advanced study or research in a given field.

fieldwork
> The work of collecting anthropological or sociological data through interviewing and observing people in their natural environment.

linguistics
> The science of language.

mentor
> A wise and trusted advisor or guide.

nuclear family
> A family group that is made up of only the father, the mother, and the children.

physical anthropology
> A division of study that deals with the comparative study of human physical variation, adaptations, and evolution.

psychoanalysis
> A method of treating emotional disorders that requires the patient to talk about past experiences, including dreams and childhood.

social scientist
> A person who studies fields such as anthropology, sociology, psychology, or economics that deal with the institutions, activities, and structure of human society.

sociologist
> A person who studies organized groups of human beings.

SOURCE NOTES

Chapter 1. Firsts
1. Jane Howard. *Margaret Mead: A Life*. New York: Simon and Schuster, 1984. 54.
2. Margaret Mead. *Blackberry Winter: My Earlier Years*. New York: William Morrow & Company, 1972. 1.
3. Ibid. 132.
4. "Margaret Mead: Human Nature and the Power of Culture." Library of Congress. 30 Nov. 2001. 10 Dec. 2007 <http://www.loc.gov/exhibits/mead/field-samoa.html>.
5. Margaret Mead. *Letters from the Field, 1925–1975*. Ed. Nanda Anshen. New York: Harper & Row, Publishers, 1977. 39–40.

Chapter 2. Ancestors of an Anthropologist
1. Margaret Mead. *Blackberry Winter: My Earlier Years*. New York: William Morrow & Company, 1972. 57.
2. Margaret Mead. *To Cherish the Life of the World: Selected Letters of Margaret Mead*. Eds. Margaret M. Caffrey and Patricia A. Francis. New York: Basic Books, 2006. 15–16.
3. Margaret Mead. *Blackberry Winter: My Earlier Years*. New York: William Morrow & Company, 1972. 2.
4. Ibid. 22.
5. Jane Howard. *Margaret Mead: A Life*. New York: Simon and Schuster, 1984. 25.

Chapter 3. The Early Years
1. Margaret Mead. *Blackberry Winter: My Earlier Years*. New York: William Morrow & Company, 1972. 20.
2. "Margaret Mead: Human Nature and the Power of Culture." Library of Congress. 30 Nov. 2001. 10 Dec. 2007 <http://www.loc.gov/exhibits/mead/mead-shaping.html>.
3. Margaret Mead. *Blackberry Winter: My Earlier Years*. New York: William Morrow & Company, 1972. 60.
4. Ibid. 63.
5. Ibid. 29.
6. Jane Howard. *Margaret Mead: A Life*. New York: Simon and Schuster, 1984. 22–23.

7. Margaret Mead. *Blackberry Winter: My Earlier Years*. New York: William Morrow & Company, 1972. 14.

Chapter 4. The School Years
1. "Margaret Mead: Human Nature and the Power of Culture." Library of Congress. 30 Nov. 2001. 10 Dec. 2007 <http://www.loc.gov/exhibits/mead/mead-shaping.html>.
2. Margaret Mead. *Blackberry Winter: My Earlier Years*. New York: William Morrow & Company, 1972. 73.
3. Ibid. 80.
4. Ibid. 81.
5. Ibid. 81–82.
6. Patricia Grinager. *Uncommon Lives*. Lanham, MD: Rowman & Littlefield Publishers, 1999. 75.
7. Margaret Mead. *Blackberry Winter: My Earlier Years*. New York: William Morrow & Company, 1972. 86.

Chapter 5. The College Years
1. Margaret Mead. *Blackberry Winter: My Earlier Years*. New York: William Morrow & Company, 1972. 97.
2. Ibid. 98.
3. Jane Howard. *Margaret Mead: A Life*. New York: Simon and Schuster, 1984. 38.
4. Ibid. 49.
5. Ibid. 43.
6. Ibid. 29.
7. Margaret Mead. *Blackberry Winter: My Earlier Years*. New York: William Morrow & Company, 1972. 114.

Chapter 6. Samoa
1. Margaret Mead. *Blackberry Winter: My Earlier Years*. New York: William Morrow & Company, 1972. 138.
2. Margaret Mead. *Coming of Age in Samoa: A Psychological Study of Primitive Youth for Western Civilisation*. New York: William Morrow & Company, 1961. 269–270.

SOURCE NOTES CONTINUED

3. Margaret Mead. *Blackberry Winter: My Earlier Years*. New York: William Morrow & Company, 1972. 152.
4. Ibid. 151.
5. Ibid. 155.

Chapter 7. The Admiralty Islands
1. Jane Howard. *Margaret Mead: A Life*. New York: Simon and Schuster, 1984. 132.
2. "Margaret Mead: Human Nature and the Power of Culture." Library of Congress. 30 Nov. 2001. 10 Dec. 2007 <http://www. loc.gov/exhibits/mead/field-manus.html>.
3. Margaret Mead. *Blackberry Winter: My Earlier Years*. New York: William Morrow & Company, 1972. 169.
4. "Margaret Mead: Human Nature and the Power of Culture." Library of Congress. 30 Nov. 2001. 10 Dec. 2007 <http://www. loc.gov/exhibits/mead/field-manus.html>.
5. Margaret Mead. *Blackberry Winter: My Earlier Years*. New York: William Morrow & Company, 1972. 206.

Chapter 8. From Bali to Baby
1. Margaret Mead. *Blackberry Winter: My Earlier Years*. New York: William Morrow & Company, 1972. 214.
2. Margaret Mead. *Sex and Temperament in Three Primitive Societies*. New York: Harper Perennial, 2001. 221–222.
3. Margaret Mead. *Blackberry Winter: My Earlier Years*. New York: William Morrow & Company, 1972. 219.
4. Ibid. 209.
5. Ibid. 249.

Chapter 9. Grandmother of the Global Village

1. The Institute for Intercultural Studies. 16 Nov. 2007
<http://www.interculturalstudies.org/main.html>.
2. "Margaret Mead: 1901–1978." Time.com. 27 Nov. 1978.
10 Dec. 2007 <http://www.time.com/time/magazinearticle/
0,9171,916486,00.html>.
3. "Margaret Mead Today: Mother to the World." Time.com.
21 Mar. 1969. 10 Dec. 2007 <http://www.time.com/time/
magazine/article/0,9171,839916-1,00.html>.
4. Ibid.
5. Melvin Maddocks. "A Most Famous Anthropologist." Time.com.
27 Aug. 1984. 10 Dec. 2007 <http://www.time.com/time/
magazine/article/0,9171,926845,00.html>.
6. Wilton S. Dillon. "Margaret Mead and Government." *American
Anthropologist* vol. 82, 1980:319–390. 1980
<http://www.publicanthropology.org/TimesPast/MeadAA.htm>.
7. Jane Howard. *Margaret Mead: A Life*. New York: Simon and
Schuster, 1984. 14.
8. Ibid. 424.

INDEX

ABOUT THE AUTHOR

Ruth Strother has been in the publishing industry for more than 20 years. She has written and edited numerous award-winning nonfiction and fiction books for children and adults. Ruth grew up in Minneapolis, Minnesota, and has spent the last 12 years trying to warm up in southern California, where she lives with her husband, daughter, and two Labs. She is the author of *Bill Gates* in the Essential Lives series.

PHOTO CREDITS